DIANA

DIANA

H.R.H. THE PRINCESS OF WALES

TIM GRAHAM

INTRODUCED BY CLIVE JAMES

MICHAEL O'MARA BOOKS LIMITED

For my wife Eileen with much love

CONTENTS

INTRODUCTION
BY
CLIVE JAMES

WHAT IS THE SECRET of his fascination? Something about Tim Graham stirs the Princess of Wales to her depths. In the nicest possible way, she is well aware that she is a dish. Even when she minds, she doesn't find it exactly *inappropriate* being snapped up at several hundred frames a second by twenty men running backwards with their camera bags tangled. But there are few photographers she will go all the way off guard for, and only one for whom she turns on the torch every time. It isn't so much that she trusts him. It's that she can't help herself. Because he *knows* she can see it in his eyes. He knows that in moments of stress she trims her fingernails with her teeth. He knows about her *nose*; that it is not petite. He even knows about that single incipient spot, right in the middle of her chin, which starts feeling like Vesuvius if she so much as looks at an ice-cream. The message of Tim Graham's understanding smile is that if the pimple comes up, it will be no disaster; it will only provide yet further proof that she is flesh and blood, very tastefully arranged. How did he manage this profound spiritual contact with the world's most wary female? The answer is simple. He doesn't catch her unawares. She knows what he is after: a moment which will encapsulate the central, absurd fact that she has been given so much prettiness to look after in one body.

She is married to a very nice, interesting man with excellent career prospects. But these privileges are paid for with a crushing round of duties, during which she meets plenty of people who conspicuously lack an advantage conferred on her as a gift from heaven, unearned, unjustifiable, a pure accident.

Beauty. What a break. Really, deep down, it's a bit of a joke, and is a joke Tim Graham gets. He gets it right in the middle of the frame.

When the seven foot Diana stands on the Australian Beach with what looks like the membership of a special club for short life-savers, naturally it's a laugh (p. 122). But he can also make her laugh at her own loveliness.

The hands-on-hips picture, the one where she is shaking with laughter inside the white blouse with the black splodges, is already a modern icon (p. 59). And it wasn't even posed: it's a candid. 'This is a real girl in a real place', said Philip Larkin about the photograph in his poem. All Tim Graham's photographs of his top model say that about her. *That's* his secret.

Clive James
April 1988

DIANA: H.R.H. THE PRINCESS OF WALES

THE PRINCESS OF WALES must have the most famous smile in the world, one that I have photographed a thousand times. Nevertheless, when I first met her all my efforts to coax a smile from her, or even a grin, failed. That was in September 1980. Lady Diana Spencer, then only 19 years old, was being linked romantically with the Prince of Wales. There had been many girlfriends in his life over the past few years, but this time the insiders felt an engagement was on the horizon. Naturally the pressure on young Lady Diana became very intense and, in an effort to appease the press, she agreed to pose for photographs at the kindergarten where she worked on that day in September 1980.

I didn't realize it when I arrived at the kindergarten, but earlier that day Lady Diana had innocently posed for newspaper photographers with her back to the sun. Her summer skirt was so flimsy the sun had made it transparent and the rather revealing photographs that resulted were on the front page of every newspaper the following day. Although Lady Diana agreed to my taking some colour pictures she was, as the photographs show, a shy and rather apprehensive subject. I remember her as a typical teenage girl: she seemed to be pretty but, with her eyes fixed firmly on the ground and her rather solemn expression, it was hard to tell.

People often ask me if I foresaw, in those early days, just how she would come to dominate the pages of the world's press. I would love to be able to say I did but that would be untrue. I had no idea, nor did anyone else, that she would become so astonishingly popular. How could anyone predict that this shy teenager would become the very epitome of glamour around the world?

After those first pictures in September, the interest in Lady Diana continued as the rumours of her romance with Prince Charles persisted. But the 'royal romance' was, in the early days, a photographer's nightmare. I tried and failed, along with everyone else, for what seemed to be forever to get a photograph of Prince Charles and

Lady Diana together. And on her own Lady Diana earned the name 'shy Di' for her knack of looking at her shoes whenever a photographer appeared.

A few weeks before the engagement was announced, as I was driving down Constitution Hill, I saw Lady Diana in her red Mini Metro heading in the opposite direction. The pressure for a good picture of her was so great by then that I did a quick U-turn and followed her car to Belgrave Square. Just as I was beginning to feel slightly foolish for chasing her around London in this way, her car pulled over and a girlfriend who was a passenger in her car came back to ask what I wanted. Rather surprised, I replied that I thought an engagement announcement was likely soon and I'd like an up-to-date picture. The friend returned to the car and came back to me to say that they were going to lunch but would be at Lady Diana's flat at a certain time and I could have a picture of her arriving there.

This incident took place only a few short months after that day at the kindergarten but it showed, in retrospect, that Lady Diana had already decided that if it was impossible to escape the glare of publicity she could at least understand it and try to control it.

Shortly after came the announcement of the royal engagement. Having had a tip-off the night before that the announcement was to be the next day I set off in the morning to see if I could get a picture of Lady Diana leaving her flat or maybe—as it was to be a big day for her—her hairdressers! I was photographing Lady Diana's father and step-mother at their London flat when my office tracked me down to say I had to get to Buckingham Palace for a 3 pm photocall with the newly engaged couple.

When Prince Charles and Lady Diana came out onto the terrace at Buckingham Palace they looked so happy but perhaps a bit self-conscious facing the press together for the first time. However, I was more nervous than they were. I knew the world's press were clamouring for these pictures and, in order to get a good picture I needed them both to look into my lens at the same time. Fortunately, this happened and when I framed the picture in my lens I let the motor-drive run. The noise startled Lady Diana who jokingly accused me of showing off. This photograph became a favourite of the royal couple who ordered copies for their personal use. The same picture was selected for the commemorative postage stamp issued in 22 Commonwealth countries.

Now on many occasions when the press is present the moment the Princess smiles or even lifts her head there is a staccato burst of dozens of motordrive cameras. It still seems slightly ridiculous to her but she has now learned to anticipate it to the point where she calls the tune. This was demonstrated when the Princess was making a speech during the recent Bicentennial visit to Australia: as she lifted her head from her notes the motordrives fired; further into the speech she lifted her

head again—the motordrives whirred. The third time she did it so deliberately that everyone burst into giggles—the Princess and the cameramen included.

If the Prince and Lady Diana thought the pressure on them would abate after the engagement was announced they were badly mistaken. If anything, the hunger for new pictures of Lady Diana increased. It seemed like a form of international hysteria at the time and I was caught up in the madness almost as much as Lady Diana.

The most extreme example of this was an evening when we were having a dinner party at our home in London. At 10 p.m. we had a 'phone message that there was to be a photocall with Prince Charles and Lady Diana at Balmoral the following morning at 9.30. The first flight to Aberdeen airport departed just after 7.00 a.m. and arrived an hour and a half later at 8.30. Balmoral was at least an hour's drive from Aberdeen airport so there was a good chance I might miss the photocall. The only answer was to get into my car and head north. My wife, Eileen, and I shared the driving and we covered the 500 miles in plenty of time for the photocall which started at 9.30 on the dot and was over at 9.35. We then got back into the car and headed south for London. A thousand miles of driving for a five minute picture session! Nevertheless, I was very pleased with the pictures which were published throughout the world.

The engagement was for Lady Diana what one might call the 'sink or swim' period. Looking back, it seems unthinkable that so much pressure could be put on one so young and inexperienced. The mitigating factor is that no one could have predicted the extent of that pressure since it was without precedent. Once, just before the wedding, when Lady Diana was at a polo match in Tidworth to watch Prince Charles compete, the strain began to show. Waiting for the prizegiving all eyes were on the royal bride-to-be. Photographers were in position in the front row and it was said at the time that they reduced her to tears. But it was not just the photographers—she had coped with larger crowds of them before—it was the public rushing forward to stare that proved too much for her. In those few tense moments she had a glimpse of an inescapable and intimidating part of her future. It is understandable that she felt so vulnerable and allowed those feelings to show.

Only two months after this low point, on 19 August, 1981, the Princess of Wales posed with her husband on the banks of the River Dee. Attractively tanned after their honeymoon cruise she was a picture of self-confidence. When the photographers presented her with a bouquet of flowers she accused them jokingly of claiming back the money on their expenses. It was as if she had been doing this sort of thing for 20 years. She looked slimmer and she had a new hairstyle but for me the important difference was the radiant smile which came so easily to her face. She was happy and all the media attention in the world could not change that. Curiously it was during the honeymoon, when she was away from the public gaze, that she had come to terms with her new life. It was as if she had decided that since she was going to be the focus of so much attention she might as well look good and try to enjoy it. She changed from passive to active; from negative to positive in this short time. As she has said since, 'There was so much attention on me when I first arrived on the scene and I wanted to get my act together.'

She must have begun 'getting her act together' on the wedding day itself. Before then she could have been forgiven for thinking that the interest in her was merely hyped up by the press, that she was 'flavour of the month' and an easy way of selling newspapers. But on their wedding day I think she and her husband found that feelings ran deeper and were more genuine than that. Prince Charles described his emotions at the time as follows: 'All night people were sitting out on the steps there singing "Rule Britannia" and every kind of thing . . . I found myself standing in the window with tears pouring down my face.'

I am sure these emotions must have been equally felt by his bride. It was the realization that her future role was more than as an item in a gossip column, although that was an annoying part of it. She would have realized then that her life had become a part of the lives of millions of people, most of whom she would never meet. The way she dealt with people, the way she dressed, the way she brought up her family would be of great interest to them all. I think she grasped this idea in those few weeks away on her honeymoon and came back ready to do the job ahead of her.

It is the style with which she has done the job which makes her so popular. Whether crouching down for a word with a shy child, sitting on the bed to chat to a hospice patient, rubbing noses to greet a Maori or laughing as a student kisses her hand, she is a joy to photograph. She has an obvious charm and a natural response to people that creates an atmosphere of warmth and friendliness wherever she goes. She uses her well known eye for fashion in some very clever ways: for example, on a visit to Japan in 1986 she wore a dress of dramatic red spots on a white background which mirrored the Japanese flag, a gesture enormously appreciated by the Japanese. She once said, 'sometimes I can be a little outrageous, which is nice.' She showed this on that same tour of Japan when she wore an extraordinary jewelled headband for a banquet with Emperor Hirohito.

Occasionally the Princess is criticized for the extravagance of her wardrobe. On the other hand there were howls of outrage from the press when she wore an 'old' gown to La Scala in Milan, so she cannot win either way. I think people want to see the Princess in glamorous outfits and I am sure she knows this. Questioned on the extent of her wardrobe, she responded, 'My clothes are for the job.'

In 1982 I had an invitation from the Prince of Wales' Press Secretary to photograph the Prince and Princess with their six-month-old-son, Prince William. A few months previously I had done my first 'private' session with Prince Edward and apparently the session went well enough to earn a return engagement. I went to the Palace the day before to see the room where I would be taking the pictures and to arrange the lighting. On the day, I began with some formal shots and then let the session develop along its own lines. If it can be said that photographers have a style then mine is informal. I aim to capture people as they are in their own surroundings rather than create an image. Once I start working I am absolutely preoccupied with my subject and my camera. I answer questions but in such an abstracted way that I am sure people must think I am an idiot. I'd had very little sleep the night before—it was the first night at home for our newborn daughter. Nevertheless, the session went well; the royal couple were in a relaxed mood and happily entered into the spirit of things. They were sympathetic too about my sleepless night.

I got a lovely shot of Prince William lying on the floor on his tummy. In the picture he is smiling broadly showing off two brand-new teeth. The reason for his smile was that his mother was on the floor next to me rattling my light meter. I was so absorbed by the job in hand it didn't seem in any way strange to be down on the floor with the Princess of Wales and a future king.

Later, for her own portrait Princess Diana was leaning on the back of a chair as I took a very tight close-up of her face looking straight into the camera with a broad and very real smile. The Princess commented when I showed her the photographs that she hadn't realized how 'close-up' the picture was going to be. However, her complexion is perfect so she has little to fear from such close scrutiny.

The Princess understands the requirements of photography quite well. She has shown me some of her own snaps of her young family and they are very competently done, with a nice eye for a composition. It is good for photographers in general that she understands our problems and it has been very useful to me because in 1985, in connection with a TV venture supported by the royal couple, from which profits were to benefit The Prince of Wales' Charities Trust, I was given the opportunity of photographing them both on duty and off duty over a period of several months. The pictures I took at that time appeared in two books written by Alastair Burnet, 'In Person' and 'In Private—In Public, The Prince and Princess of Wales'.

I was struck first of all at how easy-going the Princess was about this intrusion into her privacy. To be photographed on public occasions is one thing but to have a camera follow you into your garden, your house, your sitting-room, even your children's nursery is quite another. She was easy to work with: very cooperative whereas the 'greats' of showbusiness or politics can be very difficult. The difference is, she is very confident about her public image and she can afford to be natural. One day at Highgrove, the couple's country house in Gloucestershire, a helicopter of the Queen's Flight had arrived and the royal children were clambering in and out of it at the invitation of the crew. The Princess accepted their invitation for a chance to try out the navigator's seat and the day's pictures were a very unusual set. I couldn't resist asking for one last picture of the Princess in her garden. The result was one of my favourites with Princess Diana sitting on the grass leaning against a sundial and smiling into the camera. Even though the picture is posed, it works beautifully because she is so natural and relaxed before the camera.

This book is to be published on Princess Diana's 27th birthday, seven years after her arrival on the royal scene. The pictures are arranged chronologically and I hope they show just how dramatically that shy teenager of 1980 has taken on her new role and developed her own style—a brilliant combination of dignity and glamour hugely successful in global terms. I think they show a woman who has learned to deal with the camera in a way that no one has done before. They show a woman who, while fulfilling her role as wife of the heir to the throne, has had to deal with a world which often treats her as a pop star.

This side of her life was shown very clearly during her visit to America in 1985. On the way to a church in Washington a large group of teenage girls screamed, in a scene reminiscent of Beatle-mania, when the Princess passed by. I heard one of them, who can only have caught a fleeting glimpse of her, shriek, 'Nothing can compare to this'! It is this sort of adulation from total strangers that must be most difficult to deal with. It is the sort of pressure which has proved to be too much for many a pop star or movie idol. Yet the Princess of Wales takes it all in her stride. She manages to fulfil the fantasy images of teenagers around the world and at the same time carry out the serious work of a member of the Royal Family. These two facets of her life often overlap: more than 30 charities and campaigns such as Help the Aged, Barnardo's, Birthright, the campaign against drug abuse, and the world of ballet and music, have benefited not only from her individual efforts but enormously from the worldwide publicity she attracts to their cause.

One moment, above all, sums up for me the appeal Princess Diana has which reaches far beyond mere stardom. It was a White House banquet in 1985; she wore an off-the-shoulder, long black velvet gown which looked sensational. President Reagan had collected a glittering array of the famous, including many Hollywood stars. America had set out to dazzle the world but everyone agreed, not just the proud British, that the Princess of Wales outshone them all.

Tim Graham

1981

top TETBURY; *above* BROADLANDS; *opposite* BALMORAL

opposite TIDWORTH; *above left and right* COWDRAY PARK

above left ST PAUL'S CATHEDRAL; *above right* H.M.Y. BRITANNIA, GIBRALTAR

above right BALMORAL

opposite CARMARTHEN, WALES; *above* VICTORIA AND ALBERT MUSEUM

CARDIFF

1982

opposite BARBICAN, LONDON; *above* WINDSOR

POLO AT WINDSOR

LEAVING ST. MARY'S HOSPITAL WITH PRINCE WILLIAM

FUNERAL OF PRINCESS GRACE, MONACO

'E.T.' PREMIERE, LONDON

WREXHAM, WALES

CATFORD, LONDON

ROYAL OPERA HOUSE, LONDON

1983

opposite WITH PRINCE WILLIAM, KENSINGTON PALACE; *above* KENSINGTON PALACE

opposite SYDNEY, AUSTRALIA;
above left TAURANGA, NEW ZEALAND ; *above right* BRISBANE, AUSTRALIA

EDMONTON, CANADA

POLO MATCH, SYDNEY, AUSTRALIA

above and opposite AYERS ROCK, AUSTRALIA; *overleaf* ALICE SPRINGS, AUSTRALIA

AUCKLAND, NEW ZEALAND

opposite MASTERTON, NEW ZEALAND; *top* MELBOURNE, AUSTRALIA;
above GISBORNE, NEW ZEALAND; *overleaf* AUCKLAND, NEW ZEALAND

above 'OCTOPUSSY' PREMIERE, LONDON; *opposite* POLO AT CIRENCESTER

NEWFOUNDLAND, CANADA

1984

opposite OSLO, NORWAY; *above* ROYAL ACADEMY, LONDON

opposite POLO AT WINDSOR; *above* LEAVING ST MARY'S HOSPITAL WITH PRINCE HENRY

opposite SHREWSBURY; *above left* EALING, LONDON; *above right* BRISTOL

SOUTHAMPTON

1985

above CARDIGAN; *opposite* CAMBRIDGE

opposite ROME, ITALY; *above left* '2010' PREMIERE, LONDON; *above right* FLORENCE, ITALY

left THE VATICAN; *right* LA SPEZIA, ITALY

above right MILAN, ITALY; *overleaf* ANZIO, ITALY

POLO AT CIRENCESTER

'LES MISERABLES' AT THE BARBICAN, LONDON

BELFAST

MACEDON, AUSTRALIA

top right LONDON; *above right* MACEDON, AUSTRALIA

opposite and top ST JOSEPH'S HOSPICE, LONDON;
above WITH THE ROYAL HAMPSHIRE REGIMENT, WEST BERLIN

WITH THE ROYAL HAMPSHIRE REGIMENT, WEST BERLIN; *opposite* ROYAL FLIGHT TO AUSTRALIA

WASHINGTON, USA

ARLINGTON CEMETERY, USA

'BACK TO THE FUTURE' PREMIERE, LONDON

1986

1986

above left VANCOUVER, CANADA; *above right* NORTHAMPTON; *opposite* WINDSOR

KYOTO, JAPAN

POLO AT WINDSOR; *overleaf* 'BIGGLES' PREMIERE, LONDON

HIGHGROVE

above right SUFFOLK AGRICULTURAL ASSOCIATION SHOW

FASLANE, SCOTLAND; *opposite* OMAN

opposite BAHRAIN; *top* QATAR; *above* RIYADH, SAUDI ARABIA

SAUDI ARABIA

1987

TOLEDO, SPAIN

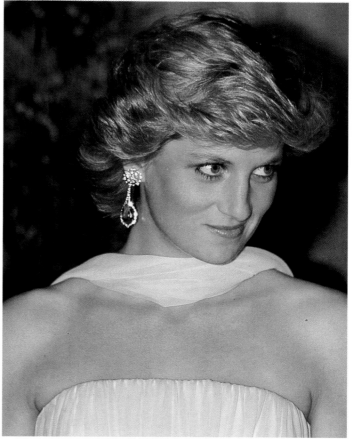

top right EL PARDO PALACE, MADRID, SPAIN; *above right* CANNES, FRANCE

top POLO AT WINDSOR WITH PRINCE HENRY; *above* THE DERBY, EPSOM

top POLO AT WINDSOR WITH PRINCE WILLIAM; *above* MAJORCA, SPAIN WITH PRINCE HENRY

HILLINGDON; *opposite* THE ROYAL OPERA HOUSE, LONDON

opposite HAMBURG, GERMANY; *above* BONN, GERMANY; *overleaf* MUNICH, GERMANY

MUNICH GERMANY

1988

SURF CARNIVAL, TERRIGAL BEACH, NEAR SYDNEY, AUSTRALIA

top right MELBOURNE, AUSTRALIA; *above right* SYDNEY, AUSTRALIA

opposite TEMPLE OF EMERALD BUDDHA, BANGKOK, THAILAND; *above* BANGKOK, THAILAND

First published in Great Britain by Michael O'Mara Books
Limited, 20 Queen Anne Street, London W1N 9FB, 1988

British Library Cataloguing in Publication Data

Graham, Tim, *1948–*
  Diana.
  1. Great Britain. Diana, Princess of
  Wales—Biographies
  I. Title
  941.085′092′4

ISBN 0-948397-87-X

Designed by Simon Bell

Typeset by Florencetype Ltd, Kewstoke, Avon
Printed and bound by Printer Industria Grafica SA, Barcelona, Spain